Editor
Gisela Lee, M.A.

Managing Editor
Karen J. Goldfluss, M.S. Ed.

Editor-in-Chief
Sharon Coan, M.S. Ed.

Illustrator
Howard Chaney

Cover Artist
Barb Lorseyedi

Art Director
CJae Froshay

Art Coordinator
Kevin Barnes

Imaging
Temo Parra

Product Manager
Phil Garcia

Publisher
Mary D. Smith, M.S. Ed.

Practice Makes Perfect
Math Games

GRADE 3

Author

Patricia Miriani Sima

Teacher Created Resources, Inc.
6421 Industry Way
Westminster, CA 92683
www.teachercreated.com

ISBN-0-7439-3723-6

©2003 Teacher Created Resources, Inc.
Reprinted, 2006
Made in U.S.A.

Table of Contents

Introduction

The old adage "practice makes perfect" can really hold true for your child in his or her education. The more practice and exposure your child has with concepts being taught in school, the more success he or she is likely to find. For many parents, knowing how to help your children can be frustrating because the resources may not be readily available. As a parent it is also difficult to know where to focus your efforts so that the extra practice your child receives at home supports what he or she is learning at school.

This book has been designed to help parents and teachers reinforce basic skills with their children. *Practice Makes Perfect* reviews basic math skills for children in grade 3. This book contains puzzles and games that allow children to learn, review, and reinforce basic math concepts. Games and puzzles have long proved their worth as vehicles of learning. Such activities carry with them three intrinsic powers of motivation—curiosity, competition, and delight. While it would be impossible to include all concepts taught in grade 3 in this book, the following main objectives are reinforced.

- basic addition
- basic subtraction
- time
- money
- place value
- rounding

- basic multiplication
- basic division
- simple geometry
- simple fractions
- logical reasoning
- problem solving

Any of the games or activities in this book may be modified to fit the needs of your child. Rules may be changed or clues may be given. Games that are designed for two players may be played on teams, or additional score sheets may be added to accommodate more players. The important thing is for students to learn something while enjoying the game or activity.

How to Make the Most of This Book

Here are some useful ideas for optimizing the games and activities in this book:

- Set aside a specific place in your home to work on the pages. Keep it neat and tidy with materials on hand.

- Once you have cut out the spinners and number cards store and label them for easy reuse. (**Note:** Some games may require several sets of number cards, so it may be necessary to make several copies of page 43.)

- Set up a certain time of day to work on the games and puzzles. This will establish consistency. An alternative is to look for times in your day or week that are less hectic and conducive to practicing skills.

- Keep all practice sessions with your child positive and constructive. If the mood becomes tense or you and your child are frustrated, set the book aside and look for another time to practice with your child.

- Help with instructions if necessary. If your child is having difficulty understanding what to do or how to get started, work through the first steps with him or her.

- Review the work your child has done. This serves as reinforcement and provides further practice.

- Look for ways to make real-life applications to the skills being reinforced.

Game 1

Spin It!

Number of Players: 2

Concept: practicing basic addition facts

Materials: spinner (page 45), markers (coins, beans, buttons, etc.), scratch paper, pencil, game board

Preparations: Follow the instructions to assemble the spinner on page 45.

Directions: Players spin the spinner. The player with the highest number goes first. He or she spins the spinner and writes the number spun. He or she then spins again and adds the two numbers together. The equation should be written on paper. The player then places a marker on his or her game board if it appears on the board and then it is the other person's turn. (**Note:** Whether or not the number appears on a player's game board, once the two numbers have been added, it is automatically the next player's turn.) Play continues until one person has covered four numbers in a row, either across, up and down, or diagonally. In order to win, this player have an equation for each number covered.

Game Board

Player 1

0	11	2	5
4	12	13	15
10	6	8	16
9	17	18	1

Player 2

0	13	14	8
7	15	6	17
3	9	18	11
12	16	1	10

Game 2

Cover Me!

Number of Players: 2

Concept: basic addition facts, logic and problem solving

Materials: game board, two dice, 12 markers (coins, beans, buttons, etc.), paper and pencil for scorekeeping

Directions: To play the game, the first player rolls the dice. He or she can either cover both numbers shown or add them up and cover the sum. For example, if a two and a six are rolled, the player can either cover the two and the six or just the sum of eight. The same player continues rolling until he or she rolls a number that can't be used. At that time, the sum of the remaining numbers is recorded as the player's score. The board is then cleared, and it becomes the next player's turn. If all the numbers have been covered and 100 points have not been reached, the game is over and that player is an instant winner. But once a player has reached 100 points, he or she is out. Play continues until there is only one player who has not reached 100 points and that player is the winner.

Game Board

1	2	3	4
5	6	7	8
9	10	11	12
13	14	15	16

Game 3

So Sorry!

Number of Players: 2

Concept: basic addition and subtraction

Materials: number cards (page 43), game board, markers (coins, beans, buttons, etc.), bag (optional)

Preparations: Cut out number cards and place them in a bag or mix them up and place them facedown on a table. Players should be able to distinguish between their markers by using different types of them.

Directions: The first player chooses two number cards. He or she then finds either the sum or difference of the two cards and places a marker on the square. Only one square may be covered per turn. Play then passes to the next player. If a square already has another player's marker on it, it may be removed and replaced with the new marker. Number cards should be replaced after each use. The winner is the first player to cover four squares in a row.

Extension: Use three number cards at a time; cards can be added or subtracted for more possibilities.

Game Board

2	16	8	7	9	1
12	10	5	14	13	2
1	6	15	6	15	9
18	0	17	3	12	10
4	14	7	5	16	3
11	8	13	4	0	11

Game 4 🐚 🐚 🐚 🐚 🐚 🐚 🐚 🐚 🐚 🐚 🐚

The Decimal Horse Race

Number of Players: 1

Concept: adding numbers with decimals

Directions: And they're off! There's No Chance in the outside lane, Fat Chance in the middle lane, and Slim Chance in the inside lane. Who will win the derby? Add each number each horse crosses—the horse with the lowest total at the end wins!

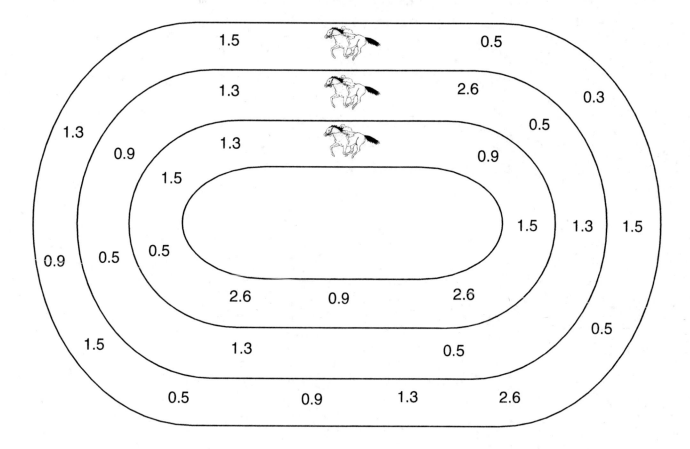

Final Count

No Chance   _____

Fat Chance   _____

Slim Chance   _____

Who will win?   _____

Game 5

Mystery Message Addition

Number of Players: 1

Concept: adding three-digit numbers

Directions: Solve each addition problem. Then find your answer in the rectangle below. The answers are all written from left to right. Cross out each correct answer. When you have finished, there will be 30 boxes that have not been crossed out. Starting with the top line and moving from left to right, write the remaining letters in order into the blank spaces at the bottom of the page. You will discover a mystery message.

1. 263 + 897	**2.** 413 + 211	**3.** 672 + 906	**4.** 433 + 572	**5.** 818 + 348
6. 196 + 508	**7.** 311 + 602	**8.** 562 + 198	**9.** 515 + 964	**10.** 749 + 510

P	H	X	L	C	A	N	B	F	F	J
1	1	6	6	3	8	9	1	4	7	9
A	I	S	T	M	T	R	A	L	O	U
6	2	4	4	7	0	4	9	0	7	6
I	P	L	P	E	M	Y	W	Z	T	O
7	6	0	0	8	1	0	0	5	4	7
D	A	Y	W	H	I	P	L	E	T	T
8	9	2	1	5	7	8	3	4	5	4
O	G	E	M	U	C	E	T	A	S	K
1	2	5	9	3	6	9	2	9	1	3
O	M	O	R	R	S	P	C	B	O	W
2	5	1	6	0	1	1	6	0	9	9

___ ___ ___ ___ ___ ___ ___ ___ ___ ___ ___ ___ ___ ___ ___ ___ ___ ___,

___ ___ ___ ___ ___ ___ ___ ___ ___ ___ ___ ___ ___ ___ ___!

Game 6 ᵒ ᵉ ᵒ ᵉ ᵒ ᵉ ᵒ ᵉ ᵒ ᵉ ᵒ ᵉ ᵒ ᵒ ᵉ ᵒ ᵉ

Mystery Message Subtraction

Number of Players: 1

Concept: subtracting two- and three-digit numbers

Directions: First solve each subtraction problem below. Then find your answer in the rectangle below. The answers are all written from left to right. Cross out each correct answer. When you have finished, there will be 19 boxes that have not been crossed out. Starting with the top line and moving from left to right, write the remaining letters in order into the blank spaces at the bottom of the page. You will discover a mystery message.

1.	89 − 34	2.	64 − 38	3.	76 − 29	4.	99 − 39	5.	58 − 17

6.	643 − 218	7.	912 − 409	8.	812 − 422	9.	447 − 291	10.	614 − 498

M 1	Q 1	S 6	C 7	T 4	A 1	H 0	R 4	S 2	D 5	I 8
T 5	A 5	L 1	I 2	T 3	E 5	R 0	H 3	O 8	D 9	A 7
A 3	M 9	P 0	Y 0	H 3	O 9	B 4	C 7	T 8	W 6	D 0
E 2	R 6	T 9	A 1	M 0	H 1	M 5	S 6	A 8	L 1	E 0

__ __ __ __ __   __ __ __ __ __ __ ,

__ __ __ __ __ __ __ __ __ __ !

Game 7 ꩜ ꩜ ꩜ ꩜ ꩜ ꩜ ꩜ ꩜ ꩜ ꩜ ꩜

Hit the Target

Number of Players: 2

Concept: addition and subtraction of two-digit numbers

Materials: spinner (page 45), two dice, paper and pencil for each player

Preparation: Follow the directions to assemble the spinner on page 45.

Directions: One player spins the spinner to determine one of the digits of the target number; the second player spins it to determine the other digit. For example, if the first player spins an eight, and the second player spins a five, the target number is either 85 or 58 (whichever the two players agree on.) The target number should be written at the top of each person's paper.

The first player rolls the dice. At the beginning of each turn, players may decide to use only one die or to use both dice. When the dice are rolled, the numbers can either be added together or used as separate digits. For example, if a player rolls a 1 and a 3, he or she can either choose 4 (the sum of one and three) or 13 or 31. This number is then written on the player's score sheet. Players take turns. After each turn, the new number is either added to or subtracted from the previous number. The first player to hit the target number wins.

Player 1

Target Number _____

Player 2

Target Number _____

Game 8

We're Equal

Number of Players: 1

Concept: addition with more than one addend, finding equal sums

Directions: Fill in the missing digits in the shapes below. The sum of the three digits in each straight line should be the same.

Extension: Use the blank shape in each row to create your own puzzle.

1.

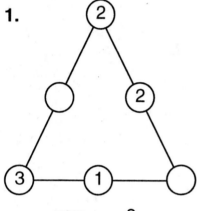

sum = ___8___

2.

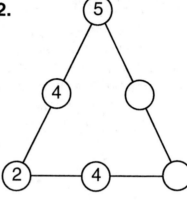

sum = _____

3.

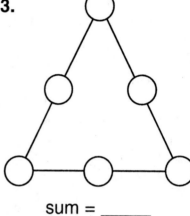

sum = _____

4.

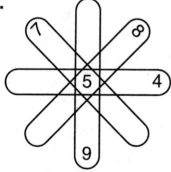

sum = ___15___

5.

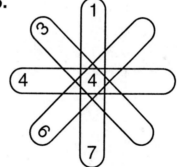

sum = ___12___

6.

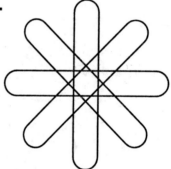

sum = _____

7.

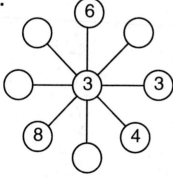

sum = ___18___

8.

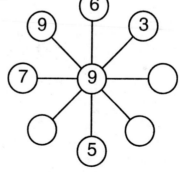

sum = _____

9.

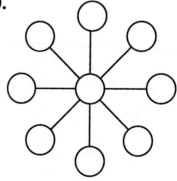

sum = _____

Game 9

Addition Show Down

Number of Players: 2

Concept: adding three two-digit numbers, problem solving

Materials: number cards (page 43), game sheet, pencil

Preparation: Cut out number cards from page 43. Players may copy the game sheet on separate paper in order to have separate sheets of paper.

Directions: Shuffle the number cards and place them facedown. Player #1 draws the top card and writes the number somewhere on his or her sheet. Then player #2 repeats the process. This continues until both players have drawn six cards and have written the numbers on their game sheets. Once a number has been written on the sheet, it cannot be changed. Both players should then find the sums of each game sheet. If there is a disagreement about the sum, a calculator may be used to determine the correct answer. The player with the greater sum is the winner.

Player One Game Sheet

Player Two Game Sheet

Game 10

How Low Can You Go?

Number of Players: 2

Concept: subtracting three-digit numbers, problem solving

Materials: number cards (page 43), game sheet, pencil

Preparation: Cut out number cards from page 43. Players may copy the game sheet on separate paper in order to have separate sheets of paper.

Directions: Shuffle the number cards and place them facedown. Player #1 draws the top card and writes the number somewhere on his or her sheet. Then player #2 repeats the process. This continues until both players have drawn six cards and written the numbers on their game sheets. But remember, make the top number bigger than the bottom number. Once a number has been written on the sheet, it cannot be changed. Both players should then find the differences of each game sheet. It there is a disagreement about the difference, a calculator may be used to determine the correct answer. The player with the smallest difference is the winner.

Note: If a player has a larger number on the second line, the other player automatically wins.

Player One Game Sheet

Player Two Game Sheet

Game 11

I Saw the Sign

Number of Players: 1

Concept: problem solving, logical reasoning, addition, and subtraction

Directions: Place + and – signs between the digits so that both sides of each equation are equal. The first one has been done for you as an example. (**Note:** Only positive, whole numbers should result when placing the signs between the digits.)

1. $8 \boxed{+} 4 \boxed{-} 3 \boxed{+} 5 \boxed{+} 2 \boxed{-} 4 = 12$

2. $9 \ \Box \ 5 \ \Box \ 6 \ \Box \ 5 \ \Box \ 6 \ \Box \ 1 = 10$

3. $3 \ \Box \ 2 \ \Box \ 7 \ \Box \ 3 \ \Box \ 5 \ \Box \ 8 = 18$

4. $5 \ \Box \ 4 \ \Box \ 8 \ \Box \ 7 \ \Box \ 4 \ \Box \ 6 = 0$

5. $2 \ \Box \ 1 \ \Box \ 3 \ \Box \ 2 \ \Box \ 8 \ \Box \ 7 = 17$

6. $4 \ \Box \ 8 \ \Box \ 3 \ \Box \ 1 \ \Box \ 5 \ \Box \ 2 = 13$

7. $1 \ \Box \ 9 \ \Box \ 7 \ \Box \ 5 \ \Box \ 2 \ \Box \ 3 = 3$

8. $6 \ \Box \ 5 \ \Box \ 8 \ \Box \ 1 \ \Box \ 5 \ \Box \ 2 = 7$

9. $7 \ \Box \ 7 \ \Box \ 4 \ \Box \ 6 \ \Box \ 3 \ \Box \ 2 = 11$

10. $9 \ \Box \ 6 \ \Box \ 7 \ \Box \ 8 \ \Box \ 4 \ \Box \ 5 = 15$

Game 12 ◔ ◕ ◔ ◕ ◔ ◕ ◔ ◔ ◕ ◔ ◕

Time Mix-Up

Number of Players: 1

Concept: telling time to the nearest five minutes

Directions: The top boxes contain analog clocks, and the bottom boxes contain the digital times. Match the clocks, then write the word from the analog clock box into the correct digital clock box. Your result will be a funny riddle.

hurty	should	to	time
(two-thirty)	tooth	what	at
you	dentist?	go	the

7:10	9:55	12:00	4:20
2:50	1:25	6:30	10:35
4:45	8:05	3:00	5:40

Game 13 ⌾ ☙ ⌾ ☙ ⌾ ☙ ☙ ⌾ ☙ ⌾

Who's Got the Time?

Number of Players: 1

Concept: common time or calendar facts

Directions: Each problem below features a number equaling some initials. If you think carefully, each formula can be translated into a well-known statement or fact about time or the calendar. An example might be 365 = D in a Y. This would represent 365 days in a year. See how long it takes you to translate them. The last three problems are a little more difficult.

1. 60 = S in a M

_____

2. 24 = H in a D

_____

3. 7 = D in a W

_____

4. 52 = W in a Y

_____

5. 60 = M in an H

_____

6. 12 = M in a Y

_____

7. 4 = W in a M

_____

8. 30 = M in a H.H.

_____

9. 28 (or 29) = D in F

_____

10. 2 = H on a C

_____

Game 14

Change It!

Number of Players: 1

Concept: finding different coin combinations to total $1.00

Materials: tally sheet, real or play money (optional)

Directions: There are over 200 ways to make change for a dollar. Use the tally sheet below to start your list. You may continue on separate paper. For fun, set a time limit and see how many ways you can make change to equal $1.00.

Extension: Instead of $1.00, use other amounts, such as 75 cents or 50 cents.

Amount $1.00

Half Dollars	Quarters	Dimes	Nickels	Pennies

Game 15 ❧ ✺ ❧ ✺ ❧ ✺ ❧ ❧ ✺ ❧ ✺

Mystery Money

Number of Players: 1

Concept: adding money, logical reasoning

Materials: scratch paper, pencil, play coins and bills (optional)

Directions: Read the problems below and write down the bills and coins used to make the designated amount.

Extension: Make up your own Mystery Money problems and give them to a friend to solve.

1. 1 bill and 5 coins equal $2.51

_____

_____

2. 2 bills and 6 coins equal $10.18

_____

_____

3. 3 bills and 7 coins equal $3.15

_____

_____

4. 4 bills and 5 coins equal $90.67

_____

_____

5. 5 bills and 9 coins equal $90.99

_____

_____

6. 9 bills equal $100

_____

_____

7. 4 bills and 6 coins equal $19.64

_____

_____

8. 5 bills and 7 coins equal $86.93

_____

_____

9. 5 bills and 2 coins equal $24.35

_____

_____

10. 4 bills and 2 coins equal $72.11

_____

_____

Game 16

Price Check

Number of Players: 1

Concept: addition and subtraction of money, making change, problem solving

Directions: Use the clues to find the price of each item. Write the correct price for each item.

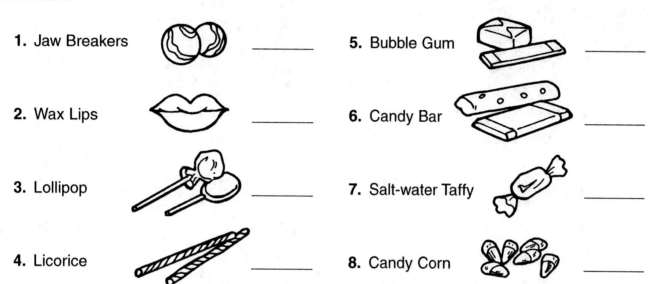

1. Jaw Breakers _____

2. Wax Lips _____

3. Lollipop _____

4. Licorice _____

5. Bubble Gum _____

6. Candy Bar _____

7. Salt-water Taffy _____

8. Candy Corn _____

- Jeff had a $5.00 bill. After he bought the candy corn, he had four $1.00 bills and a penny.

- Annie bought wax lips and bubble gum. She spent 85 cents. The wax lips are 65 cents more than the bubble gum.

- Kevin bought bubble gum and a candy bar. He spent 75 cents.

- Sarah bought 2 pieces of licorice. It cost her 16 cents.

- Sean bought a lollipop because it cost 5 cents less than the candy bar.

- Jasmine bought wax lips and salt-water taffy. She spent 90 cents.

- Miguel bought the jaw breakers, which cost 30 cents more than the salt-water taffy.

Game 17 ◑ ◔ ◔ ◑ ◔ ◑ ◑ ◑ ◔ ◑ ◔

A Maze of Money

Concept: addition of money

Directions: Find your way through the money maze. Mark the path of correct money amounts. You may go ↕ ↔ ↙ or ↘ .

$ End	7 pennies + 7 dimes = 70 cents	Start $	4 nickels + 3 dimes = 60 cents
3 pennies + 2 dimes + 2 quarters = 73 cents	4 nickels + 2 dimes + 3 quarters = $1.25	5 nickels + 1 dime + 1 quarter = 55 cents	6 pennies + 6 dimes + 1 quarter = 91 cents
8 pennies + 5 dimes = 58 cents	2 pennies + 3 quarters = 76 cents	11 pennies + 7 dimes = 78 cents	8 nickels + 3 quarters = $1.15
4 quarters + 2 dimes = $1.25	2 pennies + 6 nickels + 7 dimes = $1.02	2 nickels + 3 dimes = 45 cents	1 penny + 1 dime + 2 quarters = 61 cents
8 dimes = 40 cents	17 nickels = 85 cents	7 pennies + 5 nickels = 33 cents	10 quarters = $2.50
2 pennies + 5 nickels + 3 quarters = 87 cents	11 pennies + 4 nickels = 31 cents	3 nickels + 1 dime + 1 quarter = 45 cents	7 nickels + 7 dimes = $1.05
3 pennies + 3 dimes = 35 cents	4 pennies + 7 nickels = 39 cents	3 nickels + 3 dimes + 3 quarters = $1.20	4 pennies + 3 nickels = 19 cents

Game 18

In Your Places!

Number of Players: 1

Concept: place value to thousands place

Directions: First, decode the key by solving some simple number problems. Then, replace the icons with the correct digit and write the number it represents on the line to the right.

Key

Clue	Icon	Number
Number of cents in a nickel		
Number of planets in our solar system		
Number of teeth a baby is born with		
Number of blind mice in nursery rhyme		
Number of horns on a unicorn		
Number of sides on a stop sign		
Number of sides on a die		
Number of wheels on a bicycle		
Number of leaves on a lucky clover		
Number of dwarves in *Snow White*		

	thousands	hundreds	tens	ones	
1.	STOP	clover	baby	mouse	_____
2.	planet	unicorn	dwarf	die	_____
3.	bicycle	baby	dwarf	clover	_____
4.		unicorn	mouse	STOP	_____
5.			bicycle	clover	_____
6.	clover	die	nickel	unicorn	_____
7.	STOP	STOP	baby	clover	_____
8.			dwarf	nickel	_____
9.	nickel	unicorn	unicorn	dwarf	_____
10.	mouse	STOP	clover	bicycle	_____

Game 19 ᵔ ᵔ ᵔ ᵔ ᵔ ᵔ ᵔ ᵔ ᵔ ᵔ ᵔ ᵔ ᵔ

Lucky Place Value

Number of Players: 2

Concept: place value up to 10,000, strategy and logical reasoning

Materials: score sheet, spinner (page 45), pen or pencil

Preparation: Follow the directions to assemble the spinner on page 45.

Directions: The object of the game is to make the highest number. High numbers spun should be used in the higher place value spots, since they have more value, and low numbers should be used in the lower columns.

To play, the first player spins the spinner and writes the number in one of the place value columns. Once a number is written in a column, it may not be changed. It then becomes player #2's turn. Play continues until both players have had 5 turns. The player with the highest number is the winner.

Player 1

Game	10,000's	+ 1,000's	+ 100's	+ 10's	+ 1's
1					
2					
3					
4					
5					
6					
7					

Player 2

Game	10,000's	+ 1,000's	+ 100's	+ 10's	+ 1's
1					
2					
3					
4					
5					
6					
7					

Game 20

Round It!

Number of Players: 1

Concept: rounding whole numbers up to the ten thousands place

Directions: Follow the directions to discover a funny riddle. Round numbers below and find the answers in the answer column. The number in front of the answer tells you where to put each letter.

A 1,964 to the nearest thousand		**1.** 1,960
F 82,175 to the nearest ten		**2.** 82,000
E 7,692 to the nearest thousand		**3.** 9,300
K 82,175 to the nearest hundred		**4.** 1,000
V 1,018 to the nearest hundred		**5.** 8,000
U 82,175 to the nearest ten-thousand		**6.** 7,700
I 9,299 to the nearest ten		**7.** 2,000
Y 1,018 to the nearest ten		**8.** 1,020
R 82,175 to the nearest thousand		**9.** 80,000
L 7,692 to the nearest ten-thousand		**10.** 15,000
G 15,432 to the nearest thousand		**11.** 9,000
D 1,964 to the nearest ten		**12.** 20,000
C 15,432 to the nearest ten-thousand		**13.** 82,200
T 9,299 to the nearest thousand		**14.** 10,000
B 7,692 to the nearest hundred		**15.** 82,180

How do you __ __ __ __ __ __ __ __ __
         1   2   3   4   5   7   6   7   6   8

__ __ __ __ __ ? __ __ __ __ __ __ its
6   9 10 10   8   11   3 12 13 14   5

__ __ __ __ !
15   5   5   11

Game 21

Rounding Maze

Number of Players: 1

Concept: rounding numbers up to the nearest ten-thousand.

Directions: Find your way through the Rounding Maze. Mark the path of the correct rounding amounts. You may go ↕ ↔ ↗ or ↘ .

End	4,321 to the nearest hundred 4,400	Start	2,006 to the nearest ten 2,000
11,065 to the nearest ten 11,070	4,321 to the nearest thousand 5,000	10,237 to the nearest hundred 10,300	2,006 to the nearest ten 2,010
11,065 to the nearest hundred 11,100	4,321 to the nearest ten 4,330	4,871 to the nearest thousand 4,000	10,237 to the nearest hundred 10,200
52,916 to the nearest ten 52,910	679 to the nearest hundred 700	4,871 to the nearest ten 4,880	4,871 to the nearest ten 4,870
52,916 to the nearest thousand 52,000	679 to the nearest ten 670	32,396 to the nearest hundred 32,400	32,396 to the nearest ten-thousand 40,000

Game 22

Circles and Squares

Number of Players: 2

Concept: understanding basic multiplication facts 1–6

Materials: two dice, paper, pencil, tally sheet

Directions: Roll one die to determine who will go first. The player who rolls the higher number goes first. The first player rolls one die and draws that number of circles on the paper. He or she then rolls the second die and draws that number of squares inside each circle drawn. He or she then writes the equation the pictures represent and the product on the tally sheet. Play passes to the next player.

The game is complete after each player has had five turns. The scores are added up, and the player with the highest score wins.

Player 1

	Equation	Product
1.	=	
2.	=	
3.	=	
4.	=	
5.	=	
	Total	

Player 2

	Equation	Product
1.	=	
2.	=	
3.	=	
4.	=	
5.	=	
	Total	

Game 23

Niddy Griddy

Number of Players: 2 or more

Concept: basic multiplication facts (1–6)

Materials: grid provided below or grid paper, two dice, two crayons of different colors

Directions: Each player should select a crayon. Roll one die to determine who will go first. First player rolls two dice and colors in a rectangle on the grid to represent the multiplication problem.

For example, if a 3 and a 5 are rolled, a player may color anywhere on the grid where there is room:

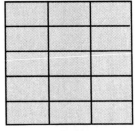

3 x 5

or

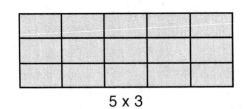

5 x 3

Players continue taking turns rolling and coloring the grid until the entire grid is filled in, or until a player is stuck and cannot color what he or she has rolled. The last player to color the grid is the winner.

Game 24

Multiplication War

Number of Players: 2

Concept: basic multiplication facts

Materials: number cards (page 43) (A deck of playing cards may be substituted.)

Preparation: Cut apart one set of number cards for each player.

Directions: This is a game for two players, and it is played similar to the card game "War." Instead of the player with the highest card taking the cards, the first player to call out the product of the two cards takes them.

To play, each player takes a card set and shuffles the cards. To begin, each player flips over the top card at the same time. The first player to correctly say the product wins both cards and puts them at the bottom of his or her deck. For example, if one player flips over a six, and one player flips over a seven, the first player to say "42" wins both cards. If both players flip over the same card, play continues as usual. The player who wins all the cards is the winner, or you may play for a predetermined amount of time, and whoever has more cards wins.

Note: If this game is played with a standard deck of cards, aces count as one, face cards are 10, and jokers are zero. Up to four players can play if a standard deck is used.

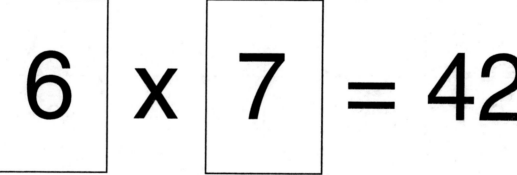

Game 25

A-Mazing Division

Number of Players: 1

Concept: basic division facts

Directions: Find your way through the Division Maze. Mark the path of the correct division amounts. You may go up ↕ ↔ ↗ or ↘ .

Start	$72 \div 8 = 7$	$16 \div 2 = 5$	**Finish**
$45 \div 5 = 5$	$56 \div 7 = 8$	$5 \div 1 = 1$	$0 \div 7 = 0$
$81 \div 9 = 9$	$36 \div 6 = 9$	$19 \div 3 = 8$	$25 \div 5 = 5$
$64 \div 8 = 8$	$32 \div 8 = 5$	$11 \div 5 = 3$	$63 \div 9 = 7$
$54 \div 6 = 9$	$12 \div 4 = 4$	$9 \div 9 = 9$	$27 \div 9 = 3$
$42 \div 6 = 7$	$9 \div 9 = 0$	$49 \div 7 = 7$	$20 \div 5 = 6$
$25 \div 5 = 6$	$24 \div 3 = 8$	$24 \div 6 = 6$	$4 \div 4 = 4$

Game 26

The Great Divide

Number of Players: 2 or more

Concept: basic division facts

Materials: 2 small objects such as coins or beans to be used as markers, two sets of number cards (page 43)

Preparation: Cut the number cards, mix them up, and place them in a bag. If no bag is available, shuffle cards and place them facedown in a pile.

Directions: Each player places his or her token on Start. Players draw a number to determine who goes first. The first player draws a card and moves his or her marker to the nearest space on the first row with a quotient that matches the number card. Then the next player takes his or her turn. With each set of turns (or a round), the players move down to the next row. During any time, if any player draws a card and there is no quotient that matches a space in a specific row on the game board, then the player loses his or her turn for that round and draws again for the next round. The first player to reach a space in the last row is the winner.

Start

$24 \div 6$	$21 \div 7$	$56 \div 7$	$63 \div 9$	$45 \div 9$	$49 \div 7$
$0 \div 5$	$7 \div 7$	$21 \div 3$	$18 \div 6$	$30 \div 6$	$81 \div 9$
$28 \div 7$	$32 \div 4$	$45 \div 9$	$48 \div 8$	$35 \div 7$	$72 \div 8$
$24 \div 3$	$4 \div 1$	$8 \div 4$	$0 \div 8$	$6 \div 6$	$35 \div 7$
$18 \div 6$	$28 \div 7$	$15 \div 3$	$32 \div 8$	$20 \div 4$	$24 \div 4$
$9 \div 3$	$0 \div 6$	$72 \div 8$	$56 \div 7$	$10 \div 5$	$1 \div 1$

Finish

Game 27

Division Anagram

Number of Players: 1

Concept: basic division facts

Directions: Solve the division facts below, and write the corresponding letters on the lines with the matching numbers.

$$\frac{\quad}{5} \ \frac{\quad}{4} \qquad \frac{\quad}{3} \ \frac{\quad}{5} \ \frac{\quad}{7} \qquad \frac{L}{10} \ \frac{\quad}{8} \ \frac{\quad}{0} \ \frac{\quad}{5} \ \frac{\quad}{1} \qquad \frac{L}{10} \ \frac{\quad}{1} \ \frac{\quad}{11}$$

$$\frac{\quad}{12} \ \frac{\quad}{9} \ \frac{\quad}{12} \ \frac{N'}{11} \qquad \frac{\quad}{0} \ \frac{\quad}{4} \ \frac{\quad}{11} \qquad \frac{\quad}{11} \ \frac{\quad}{5} \ \frac{\quad}{4}$$

$$\frac{\quad}{6} \ \frac{\quad}{7} \ \frac{\quad}{2} \ \frac{\quad}{4}$$

G $0 \div 6 = $ _____   **K** $6 \div 3 = $ _____

S $8 \div 8 = $ _____   **E** $24 \div 6 = $ _____

A $20 \div 2 = $ _____   **W** $9 \div 3 = $ _____

O $42 \div 6 = $ _____   **T** $44 \div 4 = $ _____

U $24 \div 3 = $ _____   **D** $24 \div 2 = $ _____

H $35 \div 7 = $ _____   **I** $81 \div 9 = $ _____

J $36 \div 6 = $ _____

Game 28

Stop at Bingo

Number of Players: 1

Concept: basic division and multiplication facts

Directions: Work the problems below in any order. Find your answer on the Bingo card and circle it.

Keep working on the problems until you have a Bingo, that is five circled answers in a line—up, down, or diagonally.

As soon as you find the Bingo, you can stop your work!

1. $40 \div 4 =$ _____

2. $21 \div 3 =$ _____

3. $36 \div 4 =$ _____

4. $6 \div 2 =$ _____

5. $20 \div 4 =$ _____

6. $56 \div 7 =$ _____

7. $18 \div 9 =$ _____

8. $0 \div 8 =$ _____

9. $11 \div 11 =$ _____

10. $8 \times 6 =$ _____

11. $7 \times 9 =$ _____

12. $5 \times 6 =$ _____

13. $9 \times 2 =$ _____

14. $7 \times 6 =$ _____

15. $2 \times 7 =$ _____

Bingo Card

B	I	N	G	O
8	5	30	9	64
18	11	10	1	72
48	54	15	16	0
24	70	13	63	20
3	42	14	2	7

Game 29

Division Mix-Up

Number of Players: 1

Concept: division with one-digit remainders

Directions: The top boxes contain division problems and the bottom boxes contain the answers. Solve the problems, then write the word from the problem into the correct answer box. Your result will be a funny saying.

39 ÷ 4 Venetian	36 ÷ 5 weren't	9 ÷ 4 it	11 ÷ 3 for
67 ÷ 8 be	85 ÷ 9 If	17 ÷ 6 would	44 ÷ 8 curtains
53 ÷ 7 us	25 ÷ 4 of	19 ÷ 2 all	74 ÷ 8 blinds

9 R4	2 R1	7 R1	3 R2
9 R3	9 R2	2 R1	2 R5
8 R3	5 R4	3 R2	9 R1
6 R1	7 R4		

Game 30

Am I Missing Something?

Number of Players: 1

Concept: review of basic addition, subtraction, multiplication, and division facts; problem solving.

Directions: In each shape below, there are either some operation signs or numbers missing. Start at the top and continue to the right. Write in what is missing, so that all the sides together equal the number in the middle.

1.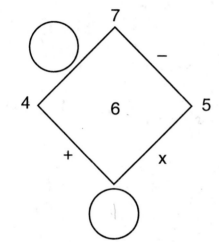

2.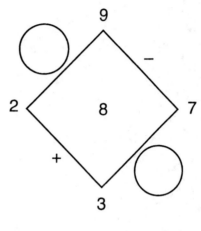

3.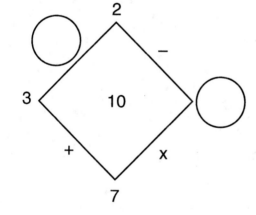

4.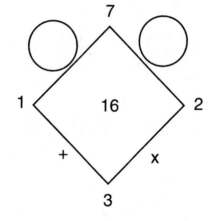

5.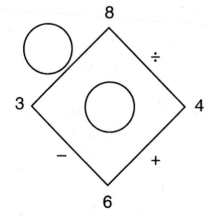

6.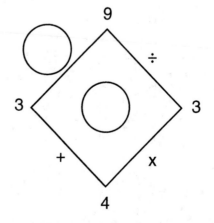

Game 31

Pizza Shop Fractions

Number of Players: 1

Concept: identifying fractions

Directions: On top of each pizza is a letter. Find the fraction below that represents the pizza and write the letter on the line that shows the correct fraction.

M

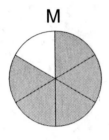

H

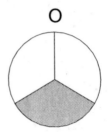

O

R

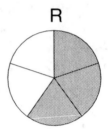

T

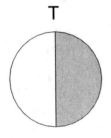

G

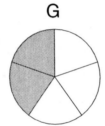

S

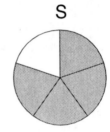

D

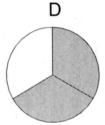

N

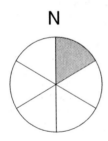

E

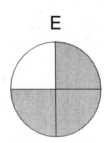

I

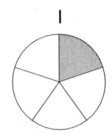

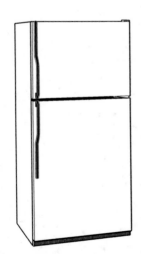

What did the ranch say to the refrigerator?

Close ___ ___ ___   ___ ___ ___ ___ ,
     $\frac{1}{2}$ $\frac{1}{4}$ $\frac{3}{4}$ $\frac{2}{3}$ $\frac{1}{3}$ $\frac{1}{3}$ $\frac{3}{5}$

___ , ___   ___ ___ ___ ___ ___ ___ ___ ___ !
$\frac{1}{5}$ $\frac{5}{6}$ $\frac{2}{3}$ $\frac{3}{5}$ $\frac{3}{4}$ $\frac{4}{5}$ $\frac{4}{5}$ $\frac{1}{5}$ $\frac{1}{6}$ $\frac{2}{5}$

Game 32

I Am the Greatest

Number of Players: 1

Concept: identifying numerators and denominators, choosing the greater fraction

Preparation: Make sure you understand that the numerator is the top number of a fraction, and the denominator is the bottom number. When comparing two fractions, if the numerators are the same, the fraction with the smaller denominator is greater.

If the denominator is the same, the fraction with the larger numerator is greater.

Directions: Each problem below contains two fractions. Write the greater fraction name on each line and then read the bold squares going down to find the answer to the riddle below.

Why didn't the bicycle want to wake up?

1. $\frac{1}{7}$ or $\frac{1}{6}$ ___ ___ _□_ ___

2. $\frac{1}{3}$ or $\frac{2}{3}$ □_ __ _____

3. $\frac{1}{12}$ or $\frac{1}{15}$ ___ _□____

4. $\frac{1}{8}$ or $\frac{1}{2}$ ___ _□_

5. $\frac{7}{10}$ or $\frac{3}{10}$ □_ _____ _____

6. $\frac{1}{10}$ or $\frac{1}{8}$ ___ ____□

7. $\frac{1}{3}$ or $\frac{2}{3}$ □_ _____

8. $\frac{1}{7}$ or $\frac{1}{4}$ ___ __□___

9. $\frac{1}{5}$ or $\frac{1}{6}$ ___ ___□_

10. $\frac{3}{7}$ or $\frac{5}{7}$ _□_ _____

11. $\frac{1}{3}$ or $\frac{1}{7}$ ___ ___□

12. $\frac{7}{9}$ or $\frac{2}{9}$ _□_ _____

13. $\frac{1}{3}$ or $\frac{1}{10}$ ___ ____□

Game 33

Symmetry Secret Message

Number of Players: 1

Concept: identifying symmetrical figures

Directions: A figure that can be folded in half so that the two halves match are symmetrical. The line that divides the two matching halves is called a *line of symmetry*.

Look at the figures below and decide if they are symmetrical. Follow the directions to reveal a secret message.

1. If figure 1 is symmetrical, put an **r** in spaces 4 and 14. If not, put an **e** in those spaces.

2. If figure 2 is symmetrical, put an **m** in space 1. If not, put a **b** in that space.

3. If figure 3 is symmetrical, put a **p** in space 10. If not, put a **c** in that space.

4. If figure 4 is symmetrical, put an **b** in space 11. If not, put an **l** in that space.

5. If figure 5 is symmetrical, put an **h** in space 3. If not, put a **k** in that space.

6. If figure 6 is symmetrical, put an **r** in space 9. If not, put a **b** in that space.

7. If figure 7 is symmetrical, put a **j** in space 8. If not, put an **i** in that space.

8. If figure 8 is symmetrical, put an **n** in spaces 6 and 13. If not, put an **f** in those spaces.

9. If figure 9 is symmetrical, put an **a** in spaces 2, 5, 7, and 12. If not, put a **u** in those spaces.

Two Wrights don't make a wrong, they

```
___  ___  ___  ___    ___  ___    ___  ___  ___  ___  ___  ___  ___  ___ .
 1    2    3    4      5    6      7    8    9    10   11   12   13   14
```

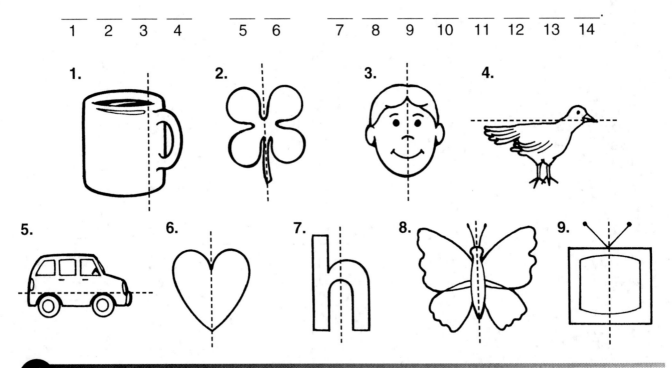

Game 34

Shape Up!

Number of Players: 1

oncept: identifying cubes, rectangular prisms, and pyramids

Directions: Look at each figure and decide if it is a cube, a rectangular prism, or a pyramid. Follow the directions to reveal a secret message.

 1. If figure 1 is a pyramid, put an **h** in space 5. If it is a cube, put an **i** in that space.

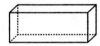 **2.** If figure 2 is a rectangular prism, put an **e** in space 10. If it is a cube, put an **h** in that space.

 3. If figure 3 is a cube, put an **l** in spaces 4 and 7. If it is a pyramid, put a **t** in those spaces.

 4. If figure 4 is a pyramid, put a **u** in space 3. If it is a rectangular prism, put an **s** in that space.

 5. If figure 5 is a rectangular prism, put an **o** in space 8. If it is a cube, put a **y** in that space.

 6. If figure 6 is a pyramid, put a **w** in space 11. If it is a cube, put an **r** in that space.

 7. If figure 7 is a pyramid, put an **a** in space 2. If it is a rectangular prism, put an **m** in that space.

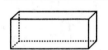 **8.** If figure 8 is a cube, put a **q** in space 9. If it is a rectangular prism, put a **w** in that space.

 9. If figure 9 is a rectangular prism, put an **n** in space 1. If it is a pyramid, put a **c** in that space.

 10. If figure 10 is a pyramid, put a **p** in space 6. If it is a cube, put an **f** in that space.

What is Lassie's favorite vegetable?

$\overline{\hspace{1em}}$ $\overline{\hspace{1em}}$ $\overline{\hspace{1em}}$ $\overline{\hspace{1em}}$ $\overline{\hspace{1em}}$ $\overline{\hspace{1em}}$ $\overline{\hspace{1em}}$ $\overline{\hspace{1em}}$ $\overline{\hspace{1em}}$ $\overline{\hspace{1em}}$ $\overline{\hspace{1em}}$
 1   2   3   4   5   6   7   8   9 10 11

Game 35

Do You Measure Up?

Number of Players: 1

Concept: measurement to the nearest 1/2 inch

Materials: ruler, pencil, paper or construction paper

Directions: Follow the instructions below to add features to the face.

1. Trace the circle pattern onto regular paper or construction paper.

2. Make the eyes 2 inches apart.

3. Draw a nose that is 3 inches long.

4. Measure your ears. Make the ears on the picture the same size as yours.

5. Make the smile 3 1/2 inches across.

6. Draw a hat that is 2 1/2 inches high.

7. Name your new friend.

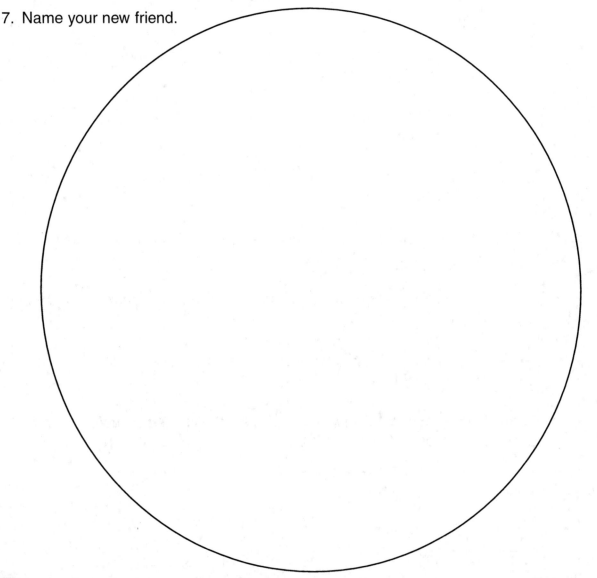

Game 36

Math Trivia

Number of Players: 2 or more

These questions may be used as replacement questions for any standard trivia game or by having the players spin the spinners and add the numbers together to determine the question number. The first player to answer 7 questions correctly is the winner.

1. What is 5 times 6? _____

2. What is 72 divided by 9? _____

3. What is 5 squared? _____

4. What is 14 rounded to the nearest 10? _____

5. What is 241 rounded to the nearest 100? _____

6. What time will it be 90 minutes after 6:00? _____

7. How many minutes are in two hours? _____

8. How many nickels are in $1.00? _____

9. How much money do you have if you have 4 dimes, 3 nickels, and 2 pennies? _____

10. What is 11 times 4? _____

11. What is 42 divided by 6? _____

12. Which is larger, 1 inch or 1 centimeter? _____

13. How many inches are in 1 foot? _____

14. How many feet are in 1 yard? _____

15. How many cups are in 1 pint? _____

16. What is the numerator in the fraction 3/5? _____

17. What is the denominator in the fraction 2/3? _____

18. If 7 out of 10 people at a party are wearing hats, what fraction of the people are wearing hats? _____

19. What fraction is greater, 3/5 or 1/5? _____

20. What fraction is greater, 5/6 or 4/6? _____

Game 36 *(cont.)*

Math Trivia *(cont.)*

21. What is the perimeter of a square that has sides that are each 3 inches long? _____

22. What is the perimeter of a triangle that has sides that are each 5 centimeters long? _____

23. Is an "+" an example of parallel lines or perpendicular lines? _____

24. Which of these is an improper fraction—3/7 or 4/3? _____

25. What is another name for 3:15 P.M.? _____

26. What is the remainder in the problem 22 divided by 7? _____

27. What is 15 plus 13 minus 7? _____

28. How many cookies are in 4 dozen? _____

29. What number is V in Roman numerals? _____

30. Is 8 a prime number? _____

31. What is 1/2 of 16? _____

32. Which is warmer, 100 degrees Fahrenheit or 100 degrees Celsius? _____

33. In the number 43,271, what digit is in the thousands place? _____

34. What is the product of 6 and 3? _____

35. What is the sum of 14 and 16? _____

36. What is the difference of 29 and 8? _____

37. What is the quotient of 15 and 3? _____

38. How many inches are in 4 feet? _____

39. How much money is 7 quarters and 2 nickels? _____

40. How many days are in 3 weeks? _____

Game 37

"Handy" Math

The only equipment needed to try these games are your hands! The number of players and concepts vary with each game.

Odds or Evens?

You need two players for this game. One player picks "odds" or "evens." This means he or she thinks the resulting number will either be odd or even. Both players put a hand behind their backs, and on the count of three, hold out any number of fingers, from zero to five. The fingers of both players are added up to see if the number is odd or even. If the guessing player was correct, he or she receives a point. It not, the other player gets the point. Players take turns guessing.

Manual Multiplication

This is a game for two players. Players put both hands behind their backs, and at the count of three, reveal one to ten fingers. The first player to correctly give the product of their fingers times their opponent's fingers receives a point. A player is not allowed to have zero fingers because the product would always be zero and they would have an advantage.

9's Multiplier

If you are having trouble remembering your 9's multiplication tables, the answer is right in front of you. Place both hands in front, palms to the wall. Starting with the pinky on your left hand, count the number of fingers you are multiplying by 9. For example, if you were doing 5 x 9, you would count five fingers, so the fifth finger would be your thumb on the left hand. Put that finger down. Next, count all the fingers before the finger that is down as tens. In this example, there would be four fingers up, or four tens, which is forty. Next, count the fingers to the right of the finger that is down as ones. In this example, there are five fingers to the right, so that is five ones, or five. Put the ones together with the tens, and you have 45 so 5 x 9 = 45!

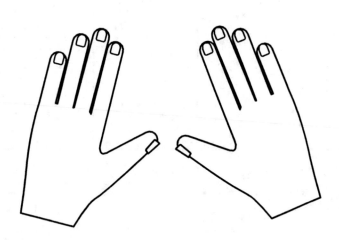

Game 38

Escape the Volcano

Number of Players: 1

Concept: review of general math concepts

Complete each math problem. Eight answers have the number 4 in them; they show the only safe way across the island to avoid the lava. Draw a line to show the way across to reach the ship.

You are here.

26 liters – 19 liters	10 x 2 ÷ 4	Number of seconds in 2 minutes	10 + 3 – 9
Number of days in 5 weeks	144 ÷ 12	Number of minutes in 3 hours	1 + 2 + 3 + 4 – 6
60 ÷ 15	45 – 32	Number of months in two seasons	32 ÷ 8
16 kg x 4	112 m + 36 m	17 – 9 – 4	$4.20 – $3.80

Number Cards

0	1	2	3
4	5	6	7
8	9	0	1
2	3	4	5
6	7	8	9

This page is blank
for cutting out objects
on page 43.

Spinner Pattern

Directions: Cut out the circle and the arrow. Attach the arrow to the circle with a brad.

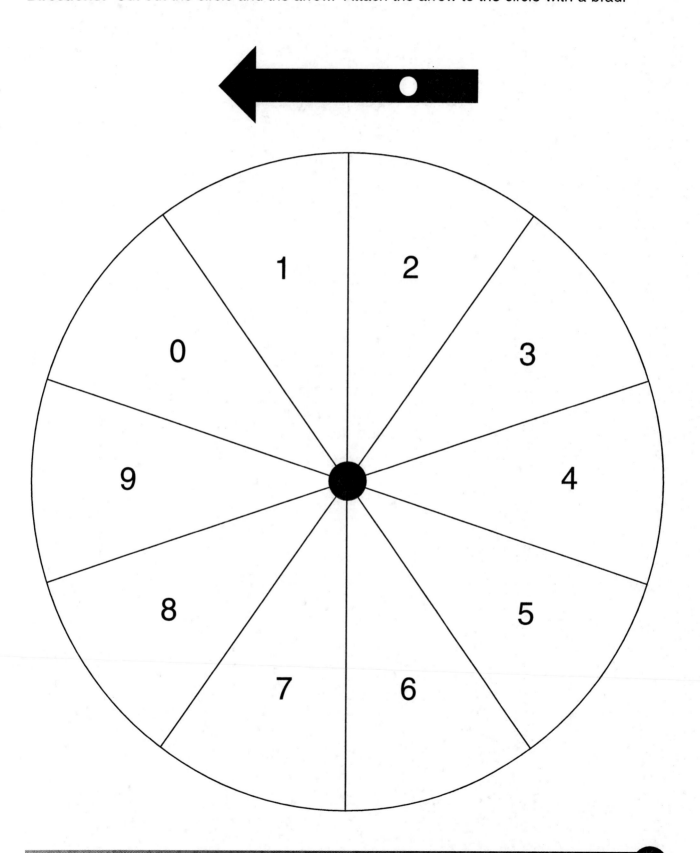

This page is blank
for cutting out objects
on page 45.

Answer Key

Page 7
No Chance–13.3

Slim chance–11.8

Fat Chance 8.9 (winner)

Page 8
1. 1,160	6. 704
2. 624	7. 913
3. 1,578	8. 760
4. 1,005	9. 1,479
5. 1,166	10. 1,259

Mystery Message: Cantaloupe Today, Lettuce Tomorrow!

Page 9
1. 55	6. 425
2. 26	7. 503
3. 47	8. 390
4. 60	9. 156
5. 41	10. 116

Mystery Message: Chili Today, Hot Tamale!

Page 11
1. 3, 4	6. Answers will vary.
2. 1, 5; sum = 11	7. 12, 11, 7, 9
3. Answers will vary.	8. 4, 2, 8; sum = 20
4. 6, 1, 3, 2	9. Answers will vary.
5. 2, 4, 5	

Page 14
1. $8 + 4 - 3 + 5 + 2 - 4 = 12$
2. $9 - 5 + 6 + 5 - 6 + 1 = 10$
3. $3 - 2 + 7 - 3 + 5 + 8 = 18$
4. $5 + 4 + 8 - 7 - 4 - 6 = 0$
5. $2 - 1 + 3 - 2 + 8 + 7 = 17$
6. $4 + 8 + 3 + 1 - 5 + 2 = 13$
7. $1 + 9 - 7 + 5 - 2 - 3 = 3$
8. $6 - 5 + 8 + 1 - 5 + 2 = 7$
9. $7 + 7 - 4 + 6 - 3 - 2 = 11$
10. $9 + 6 - 7 + 8 + 4 - 5 = 15$

Page 15
At what time should you go to the dentist? tooth hurty (two-thirty)

Page 16
1. 60 seconds in a minute
2. 24 hours in a day
3. 7 days in a week
4. 52 weeks in a year
5. 60 minutes in an hour
6. 12 months in a year
7. 4 weeks in a month
8. 30 minutes in a half-hour
9. 28 (or 29) days in February
10. 2 hands on a clock

Page 18
1. 1 $2 bill, 1 quarter, 2 dimes, 1 nickel, 1 penny
2. 2 $5 bills, 3 nickels, 3 pennies
3. 3 $1 bills, 2 nickels, 5 pennies
4. 1 $50 bill, 1 $20 bill, 2 $10 bills, 1 half-dollar, 1 dime, 1 nickel, 2 pennies
5. 4 $20 bills, 1 $10 bill, 3 quarters, 2 dimes, 4 pennies
6. 1 $50 bill, 2 $20 bills, 1 $5 bill, 5 $1 bills
7. 1 $10 bill, 1 $5 bill, 2 $2 bills, 1 half dollar, 1 dime, 4 pennies
8. 1 $50 bill, 1 $20 bill, 1 $10 bill, 1 $5 bill, 1 $1 bill, 1 half dollar, 1 quarter, 1 dime, 1 nickel, 3 pennies
9. 1 $20 bill, 4 $1 bills, 1 quarter, 1 dime
10. 1 $50 bill, 1 $20 bill, 2 $1 bills, 1 dime, 1 penny

Page 19
1. Jaw Breakers 45¢	5. Bubble Gum 10¢
2. Wax Lips 75¢	6. Candy Bar 65¢
3. Lollipop 60¢	7. Saltwater Taffy 15¢
4. Licorice 8¢	8. Candy Corn 99¢

Page 20
$ End	7 pennies + 7 dimes = 70 cents	Start $	4 nickels + 3 dimes = 60 cents
3 pennies + 2 dimes + 2 quarters = 73 cents	4 nickels + 2 dimes + 3 quarters = $1.25	5 nickels + 1 dime + 1 quarter = 55 cents	6 pennies + 6 dimes + 1 quarter = 91 cents
8 pennies + 5 dimes = 58 cents	2 pennies + 3 quarters = 76 cents	11 pennies + 7 dimes = 78 cents	8 nickels + 3 quarters = $1.15
4 quarters + 2 dimes = $1.25	2 pennies + 6 nickels + 7 dimes = $1.02	2 nickels + 3 dimes = 45 cents	1 penny + 1 dime + 2 quarters = 61 cents
8 dimes = 40 cents	17 nickels = 85 cents	7 pennies + 5 nickels = 33 cents	10 quarters = $2.50
2 pennies + 5 nickels + 3 quarters = 87 cents	11 pennies + 4 nickels = 31 cents	3 nickels + 1 dime + 1 quarter = 45 cents	7 nickels + 7 dimes = $1.05
3 pennies + 3 dimes = 35 cents	4 pennies + 7 nickels = 39 cents	3 nickels + 3 dimes + 3 quarters = $1.20	4 pennies + 3 nickels = 19 cents

Answer Key ⟳ ⟳ ⟳ ⟳ ⟳ ⟳ ⟳ ⟳ ⟳ ⟳ ⟳ ⟳ ⟳ ⟳

Page 21

1. 8,403
2. 9,176
3. 2,074
4. 138
5. 24
6. 4,651
7. 8,804
8. 75
9. 5,117
10. 3,842

Page 23

How do you drive a baby buggy?
Tickle its feet!

Page 24

End	4,321 to the nearest hundred 4,400	Start	2,006 to the nearest ten 2,000
11,065 to the nearest ten 11,070	4,321 to the nearest thousand 5,000	10,237 to the nearest hundred 10,300	2,006 to the nearest ten 2,010
11,065 to the nearest hundred 11,100	4,321 to the nearest ten 4,330	4,871 to the nearest thousand 4,000	10,237 to the nearest hundred 10,200
52,916 to the nearest ten 52,910	679 to the nearest hundred 700	4,871 to the nearest ten 4,880	4,871 to the nearest ten 4,870
52,916 to the nearest thousand 52,000	679 to the nearest ten 670	32,396 to the nearest hundred 32,400	32,396 to the nearest ten-thousand 40,000

Page 28

Start	72 ÷ 8 = 7	16 ÷ 2 = 5	Finish
45 ÷ 5 = 5	56 ÷ 7 = 8	5 ÷ 1 = 1	0 ÷ 7 = 0
81 ÷ 9 = 9	36 ÷ 6 = 9	19 ÷ 3 = 8	25 ÷ 5 = 5
64 ÷ 8 = 8	32 ÷ 8 = 5	11 ÷ 5 = 3	63 ÷ 9 = 7
54 ÷ 6 = 9	12 ÷ 4 = 4	9 ÷ 9 = 9	27 ÷ 9 = 3
42 ÷ 6 = 7	9 ÷ 9 = 0	49 ÷ 7 = 7	20 ÷ 5 = 6
25 ÷ 5 = 6	24 ÷ 3 = 8	24 ÷ 6 = 6	4 ÷ 4 = 4

Page 30

He who laughs last didn't get the joke.

Page 31

1. 10
2. 7
3. 9
4. 3
5. 5
6. 8
7. 2
8. 0
9. 1
10. 48
11. 63
12. 30
13. 18
14. 42
15. 14

Page 32

If it weren't for Venetian blinds, it would be curtains for all of us.

Page 33

1. 1
2. x
3. 1
4. –
5. 5
6. 15

Page 34

Close the door,
I'm dressing!

Page 35

It was two-tired.

Pages 39 and 40

1. 30
2. 8
3. 25
4. 10
5. 200
6. 7:30
7. 120
8. 20
9. 57¢
10. 44
11. 7
12. 1 inch
13. 12
14. 3
15. 2
16. 3
17. 3
18. 7/10
19. 3/5
20. 5/6

Page 36

Make an airplane.

Page 37

cauliflower

21. 12 inches
22. 15 cm
23. perpendicular
24. 4/3
25. quarter past 3 p.m.
26. 3 R1
27. 21
28. 48
29. 5
30. no
31. 8
32. 100°C
33. 3
34. 18
35. 30
36. 21
37. 5
38. 48
39. $1.85
40. 21

Page 42

The safe way across is 60 ÷ 15, 16 kg x 4, 112 m + 36 m, 17 − 9 − 4, $4.20 − $3.80, 32 ÷ 8, 1 + 2 + 3 + 4 − 6, 10 + 3 − 9